Liberty

by Meish Goldish
illustrated by Tom Leonard

Chapters

Harcourt
Orlando Boston Dallas Chicago San Diego
Visit *The Learning Site!*
www.harcourtschool.com

An Idea Is Born

On July 4, 1776, a great event took place: the United States was born. Until that time, the King of Great Britain had ruled over America. Now, Americans declared themselves to be free.

Their freedom did not come easily, however. Americans had to fight for it. The Revolutionary War lasted from 1775 to 1783. Finally, Britain agreed to a peace.

During the war, America was helped by other countries. One of them was France. French soldiers came to America to fight the British. They helped America win its freedom.

Many French peopled cherished their new friendship with America. They loved the idea of freedom. They wanted more freedom for themselves. They were ruled by the King of France. The king gave his people very few rights of their own.

The French people fought for more freedom. It took them ten years to win rights for themselves.

In 1865, a teacher in France had an idea. He wanted a giant statue to be built. It would be a gift from France to the United States. It would remind people how France helped the American people win freedom. It would also be a sign of friendship between the freedom-loving people of France and the United States.

The teacher told his idea to Frédéric Bartholdi, a sculptor. In 1871, Bartholdi sailed to New York. There he saw an island in New York Harbor. He felt it would be the perfect place for the statue to stand.

Bartholdi soon returned to Paris. In his workshop, he drew pictures and made models of his statue. He decided it would be a woman called Liberty. She would be a symbol of freedom.

Bartholdi had a huge job ahead of him. He wanted Liberty to be a giant statue. He wanted visitors to walk inside and climb stairs to the top. There, they could step outside and look out over New York Harbor.

What a magnificent sight that would be!

Building the Statue

The Statue of Liberty was an enormous project.

Bartholdi planned exactly how Liberty would look. She would stand proudly, wearing a long, loose robe. Her right arm would be raised high, holding a torch. Her left arm would hold a tablet with the date July 4, 1776. This date marked America's independence from Britain.

Bartholdi sculpted Liberty's face to look like his mother's. On her head would sit a crown with seven spikes. They would stand for the seven seas and seven continents. At Liberty's feet would be a broken chain. The broken chain was a symbol of freedom.

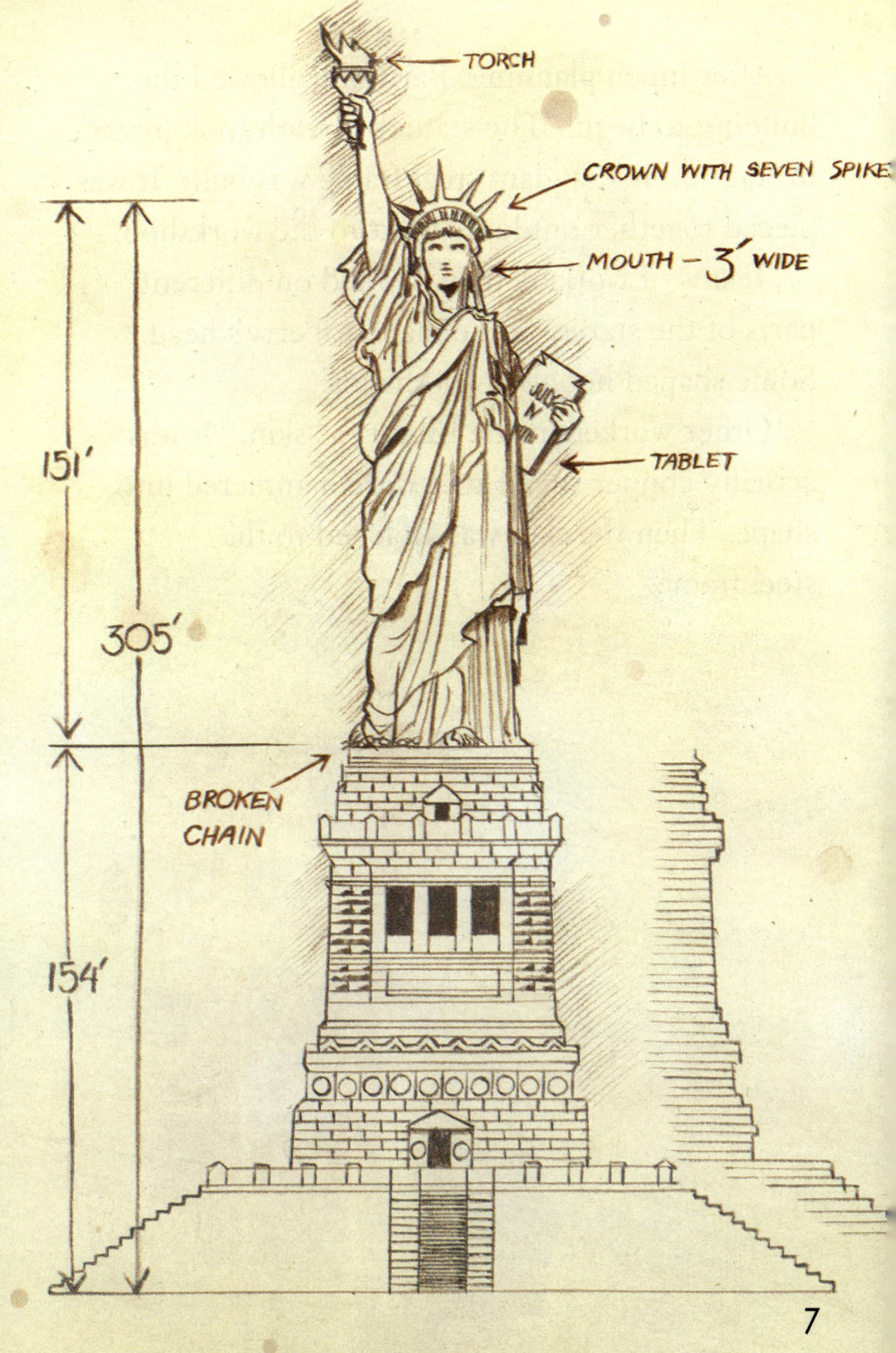
TORCH
CROWN WITH SEVEN SPIKE
MOUTH – 3′ WIDE
TABLET
151′
305′
154′
BROKEN
CHAIN

After much planning, Bartholdi allowed the building to begin. The statue's growth took place in stages. First, a giant steel frame was built. It was pieced together outdoors, next to the workshop.

Teams of workers then worked on different parts of the statue. Some made Liberty's head. Some shaped her arms and hands.

Other workers made Liberty's "skin." It was actually copper sheets that were hammered into shape. Then the skin was attached to the steel frame.

Bartholdi had hoped to finish the statue by July 4, 1876. He wanted it to be ready for America's 100th birthday. He thought there would be ample time. He was wrong. There was not enough time.

Bartholdi could send only one part of the statue to America in 1876. It was Liberty's hand holding the torch. The piece was shown at a special fair in Philadelphia. Later it was displayed in New York City.

Meanwhile, Liberty's head was shown at the World's Fair in Paris. People paid money to walk around inside. The money helped pay the cost of building the statue.

After a few years, Liberty's hand was sent back to Paris. The building of the statue continued. It was a magnificent sight. People in the streets of Paris gazed at the giant figure as it grew.

In 1884, the statue was finally finished. People from all over France came to see the gift they were giving to America. Some even walked inside and climbed the 168 steps to the crown.

At last Liberty was complete, but only half the job was done. Now the huge statue had to be sent to New York.

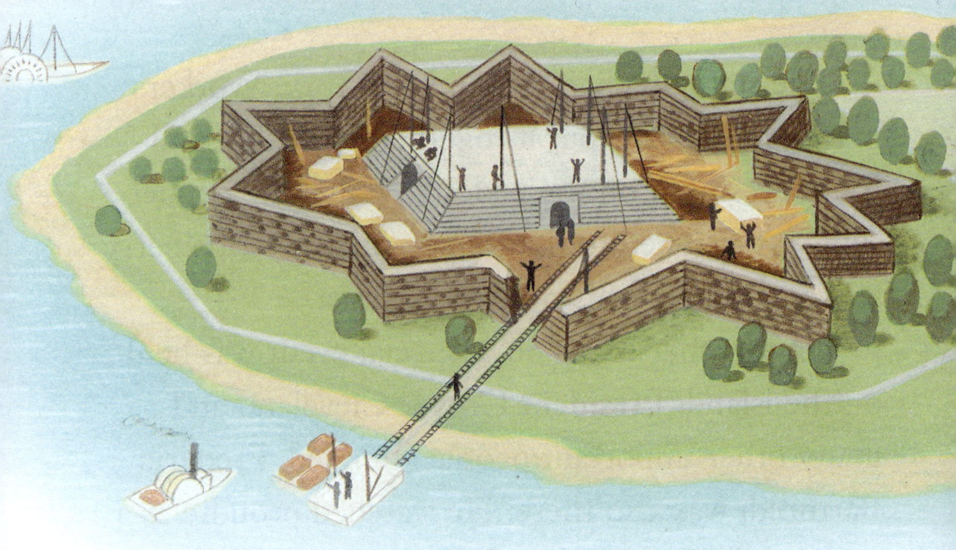

Liberty was much too large to sail to America in one piece. The statue had to be taken apart and packed into 214 crates. But there was no pedestal for the statue to stand on.

An American newspaper printed articles about the statue. The newspaper articles asked Americans to pay for a pedestal for Liberty to stand on. They did.

Now workers in New York got ready for the statue. They dug furrows and loosened the soil where Liberty would stand. Then they began to build a huge pedestal for Liberty to stand on.

More than 100,000 Americans sent in money. Many children sent in their pennies. By April 1886, the base was completed.

The statue had arrived in New York. Workers on the island now put it together. First the steel frame was built on the pedestal. Then the copper skin was fastened to the frame. Once again Liberty stood complete, this time in America.

On October 28, 1886, a special event was held on the island. President Grover Cleveland and many other important people attended. Frédéric Bartholdi was also there. He watched proudly as a parade of ships sailed by Liberty.

America had a new symbol of freedom.

The Statue Today

Today, Liberty still stands proudly in New York Harbor. For over 100 years, she has welcomed millions of people to America. She is a symbol of hope and freedom to all who see her.

The statue has seen many changes over the years. At first, it was lit up only by electric lights inside the torch. Some people feared the lights were too dim for ships to see clearly at night.

Later, very bright lights were placed at the statue's base to light it up. The lights inside the torch were also made much stronger.

By the early 1980s, the statue had grown old and needed many repairs. Once again, France and America worked together to do the job. They wanted to finish in time for Liberty's 100th birthday, in 1986.

The repairs would cost many millions of dollars. Both the French and Americans gave money, just as they had 100 years earlier.

Soon the repairs began. Workers removed Liberty's old torch. They built a new one and painted it gold. They also replaced parts of the frame, crown, and pedestal. They put a new elevator inside the statue.

After 100 years, Liberty also needed a bath. Over time, her copper skin had turned from brown to green. Workers scrubbed the inside to make the brown color return. However, they cleaned the outside very gently. They wanted to keep Liberty's now-famous green look.

Finally, all the repairs were completed and in 1986 two celebrations were held. One took place on July 4, on America's 210th birthday. The other took place on October 28, Liberty's 100th birthday. Both were happy, noisy events with many ships and plenty of fireworks.

Today Liberty stands in New York Harbor, looking fresh and new. Her golden torch shines brightly. Her light is a light of hope for all who see it. She has the light that cannot be shunned. It is the light of free people. It is the light of freedom.

Liberty can't move, as a windmill does. She can't speak, as a movie does. Yet she has moved people's hearts and spoken to their dreams for a very long time.

The Statue of Liberty began as a gift of friendship. Today, that gift keeps on giving hope to many. It continues to be a powerful symbol of freedom for America and the world.